Arlington Court

and the National Trust Carriage Museum

DEVON

A souvenir guide

THE CHICHESTER FAMILY ESTATE

Amidst the unspoilt countryside of North Devon lies the unexpected jewel of Arlington Court. It has been owned by a branch of the prestigious Chichester family since the 14th century until the last in line, Miss Rosalie Chichester, bequeathed the estate to the National Trust in 1949.

Arlington Court lies at the centre of landscaped gardens and parkland within an agricultural estate of around 2,700 acres, including 450 acres of woodland, several farms and cottages in the hamlets of Arlington, Arlington Beccott, Churchill and Loxhore.

The Chichesters of Arlington

The Chichesters were first established in Devon in 1385, when John Chichester of Somerset married Thomasia, daughter and sole heiress of wealthy landowner Sir John Raleigh, making the Chichesters one of the most important families in North Devon. This was to be one of many negotiated nuptials that would bring land, wealth and prestige to the family.

By the early part of the 16th century, the Chichesters had become such influential landowners that Sir John Chichester (1474–1537) could divide the manors between his five sons. The eldest son Edward (d.1526) inherited the family estate of Youlston (see Saxton's survey opposite), whilst Amyas (c.1512–77), being the youngest son of Sir

Right View over the parkland at Arlington Court

OPPOSITE

Top The bridge over the River Yeo on the estate

Bottom Saxton's survey of 1575

John's second marriage, received the lesser estate of Arlington.

Amyas Chichester married Joan Gifford and, with thirteen sons and four daughters, they created a solid foundation for the Arlington family, which was to remain unbroken until 1949. John Prince rather overstated the size of Amyas' family when he included them in *Worthies of Devon* (1701): 'Amias Chichester of that place, Esquire, by Joan his wife … had 19 sons, every one of which had no less than four sisters. 14 of the 19 lived to be proper gentlemen, though not above three of them had issue. When they all went to church the first would be in the church porch before the last would be out of the house.' Charles Kingsley also refers to this singular sight in his novel of 1855 *Westward Ho!*

The Tudor house and estate

When Amyas settled at Arlington there was probably some type of residential building that he either replaced or significantly extended to meet the needs of his growing family. Standing on the south side of the church and commanding beautiful views of the valley of the Yeo, the resulting Devon manor was to be the family home for more than 150 years. By the end of the 17th century the landscape was one of arable fields, meadows and woodlands interspersed over large areas of moor and heath. There were six garden enclosures bounded by the southern and northern Grove Woods together with five orchard enclosures descending the valley in the area now known as the Wilderness, suggesting that the Chichesters were making the land productive whilst also considering its ornamental and recreational purpose.

3

THE RECUSANTS

John Chichester (1602–44)

During the Civil War John Chichester remained loyal to Charles I and appears to have played an active role collecting arms for the Royalists. A letter from a West Country puritan, dated 21 October 1642, states: 'There hath been more substantial armour found in Mr Chichester's house at Arlington, and Master Courtenay his house at Molland, than in our whole county, gentry excepted. At the searching of these gentlemen's houses there were several wounded.'

John Chichester died in 1644, at a time when the Royalists had the upper hand in the region. When the Royalists were ultimately defeated, although the family was heavily penalised financially, his son and heir John Chichester, being a minor, escaped persecution and Arlington was granted a reprieve. It was young John Chichester's grandmother, Susan Playters, who paid the price for their continued support of the Roman Catholic religion. She appears in the list of Popish Recusants (see box opposite) whose property was confiscated.

Acquisition of Welsh estates

Son of John Jr, Giles Chichester (1677–1724) restored much of the family wealth that had been lost during the Civil War on his marriage to Catherine Palmer of Wingham, Kent. Catherine Palmer was niece and sole heiress to

Below Benjamin Donn's map of 1765

Right Roger Palmer, Earl of Castlemaine, (1634–1705) whose wealth – and name – passed into the Chichester family

the Castlemaine estates and brought with her large amounts of land in Cardiganshire and Montgomeryshire. Giles died leaving Arlington to his elder son, another John, then aged only seventeen. After her husband's death, Catherine retired to her Welsh property near Aberystwyth. A number of letters from Catherine to her son are held at Barnstaple Records Office. In tiny, hardly legible handwriting, Catherine offers guidance on estate and financial matters and in one of the letters, like many mothers before and since, she gently bemoans the lack of written response.

John Chichester (1707–83)

The young John inherited an estate that was at that time very much as it had been for generations. The Chichesters continued to live comfortably in the Tudor house but, although their financial status had improved, they were restricted from developing any political or high social standing within the community whilst the Recusancy Laws were still in place. It had also become increasingly difficult to marry into suitable local Catholic families. Following the death of his first wife, fourteen years his senior, John Chichester then aged 57, went further afield to Scotland to marry Mary, the daughter of Major Donald MacDonald of Tir na Dris (Terndreich), 30 years his junior. Their son and heir was christened John Palmer Chichester in recognition of the important contribution his grandmother had made to the Chichester family.

Left Heraldic shield commemorating the marriage of John Chichester to Mary MacDonald in 1764

The Recusancy

The Recusancy Laws made the Protestant faith a matter of statutory compliance. For centuries the Chichesters had been devout Roman Catholics and refused to switch allegiance following the Reformation. From 1695, when it became compulsory for births, marriages and deaths to be overseen by the Anglican ministry, Arlington's incumbent Catholic priest continued to secretly carry out the services with an Anglican minister recording the events 'ut fertu', or 'as I am told'. Given the lengths gone to in order to keep the faith, it must have caused the family considerable distress when John Palmer Chichester (overleaf) married the Protestant Agnes Hamilton and, in 1793, read his recantation in Exeter Cathedral. In his *Collections Illustrating the History of Catholic Families in Devon and Cornwall* Dr D.G. Oliver writes: '...until this unhappy defection, a priest had been maintained in the family. But after this event, the oldest chaplaincy in Devon was closed up and the last incumbent, the Rev. Henry Innes was turned adrift, to the grief of Mrs Chichester.'

THE ESTABLISHMENT

Colonel John Chichester occupies a key position in the development of the family, the buildings at Arlington and the designed landscape.

In 1790 he married Mary Anne Cary and appointed the architect John Meadows to design a fashionable Georgian mansion to replace the Tudor manor house. However, in less than a year, Meadows was dead (he is buried in the church) and the new house was completed without his supervision. Further tragedy struck at Arlington when, on 31 October 1791, a few days after giving birth to a baby daughter, Mary Chichester also died and was buried at Arlington.

Right Colonel John Palmer Chichester; portrait miniature attributed to Philip Jean, c.1790

Two years later, Colonel Chichester married Agnes Hamilton and, against family wishes, converted to the Church of England. Four sons and two daughters were born and, with the renunciation of his Catholic faith, the restrictions invoked by the Recusancy Laws were lifted and a new social era could begin.

But, less than 30 years after it had been built, the Georgian mansion was showing structural problems and Colonel Chichester took the opportunity to select a new site for a brand new building. He engaged architect Thomas Lee who designed the neo-Classical house that stands today. Colonel Chichester never had the pleasure of living in the house he commissioned, however: he died in 1823, just as building works were completed.

Sir John Palmer Bruce Chichester, 1st Bt (1794–1851)

Colonel Chichester's eldest son and heir, Sir John Palmer Bruce, known as 'Arlington Jack' by his friends, entered the navy in 1810, serving at the defence of Cadiz and the American war where he was injured in 1814 during the capture of a gun vessel. In 1820 he returned from naval duties to direct his energies at Arlington and local politics. Sir John was elected as the Liberal MP for Barnstaple in 1831 and again in 1832, 1835 and 1837.

Sir John's three brothers were also successful in their careers: George Chichester entered the army and retired in

1832 with the rank of Major; Robert Bruce Chichester was called to the Bar and was appointed Revising Barrister for the county of Gloucester; and the Reverend James Hamilton John Chichester became Rector of Arlington in 1824, when the old rectory was replaced with a stylish and spacious home, Glebe House, also designed by Thomas Lee.

Sir John was 44 when he married Caroline Thistlethwayte, by whom he had a son and a daughter. In 1840 he was created a baronet. With their contemporary and fine taste, the home commissioned by Colonel Chichester was decorated and furnished to the highest standard. Of the original decorations only three schemes now survive: the Morning Room, Ante Room and Boudoir.

Above St James's church and Old Arlington Court, built by Colonel Chichester around 1790 and demolished only 30 years later; by Maria Pixell (The Chichester Collection)

Right Agnes Hamilton, Mrs John Palmer Chichester; portrait miniature attributed to Andrew Plimer, c.1790

THE LEISURED CLASSES

Sir Alexander Bruce Chichester, 2nd Bt (1842–81)

The son of Sir John and Lady Caroline was born in Malta on Christmas Eve in 1842 and inherited the estate at just nine years of age. Sir Bruce, as he would come to be known, married Rosalie Amelia Chamberlayne in 1865 and the couple honeymooned on one of Sir Bruce's yachts, the *Zoë*, sailing from Malta for a Mediterranean cruise.

This was the height of the Victorian era and Sir Bruce enjoyed the lifestyle of a young society gentleman whilst fulfilling his role as responsible local landowner. He was a captain in the North Devon Yeomanry, but still found time to play cricket for the Arlington XI and in 1864 built a new stable block for his hunters. By 1868 the house had doubled in size with the addition of an enlarged staircase hall, new dining room and service wing.

Sir Bruce and Lady Chichester's only child, Rosalie Caroline, was born at the end of the year in which they married, and when she was only three years old they took her on her first Mediterranean cruise. It was during the second of such lengthy cruises, at the age of twelve, that Rosalie recorded: 'Wednesday January 23rd ... went on shore to the Chiaja with Miss Berners. Papa too ill for Mama to leave him….' Sir Bruce was never to fully recover from 'Maltese fever' (brucellosis). After a rainy day spent hosting a church bazaar in the grounds at Arlington, he contracted a chill and died soon afterwards, short of his 39th birthday.

Two years later Lady Chichester married a distant cousin, Sir Arthur Chichester of Youlston. Yet she continued to spend most of her time at Arlington, where she and her daughter commenced the long and arduous task of paying off the debts that had accumulated during Sir Bruce's short but flamboyant lifetime.

Left Rosalie Chichester and her mother Lady Chichester around 1870

Right Sir Bruce in his uniform as a captain in the North Devon Yeomanry

THE DIARY OF A CHILD, 1877–78

Miss Rosalie Chichester accompanied her parents on two Mediterranean cruises, the first when she was three and the second when she was twelve. This extract is taken from the diary she kept on the second of those cruises from 8 November 1877 to 13 June 1878. It provides an interesting insight into life aboard the yacht *Erminia* and the excitement of a child experiencing a storm at sea. The image shown is in fact Sir Bruce's yacht the *Zoë* in similarly storm-tossed seas.

Friday 21st December 1877. Last night about 12 o'clock I woke hearing the sailors reefing the mainsail and taking the jib down. A lot of calling and the wind roaring and whistling. Then my soap dish cover gave a jump and fell breaking to the ground, for the ship was jumping. My bed – a swinging one – was screwed up. Papa came in and asked if I would like it undone, but I did not. I then rolled from side to side and up and down again. It was good fun. My chair took a walk across my room. After a time it fell over, all my clothes on it fell about. I had to call Smith to undo my bed, then it swung so far that I could not go farther. I jumped out of bed to peep in the main cabin; I never saw anything like it, the books were all over the ground, a chair tumbled over. After a little, fell asleep. Woke up and saw my toilet cover off the chest of drawers, books, work etc. strewn about. No-one could stand. Got on deck, but dared not move.

UNDER NEW MANAGEMENT

Miss Rosalie Caroline Chichester (1865–1949)

Difficult decisions had to be made following the death of Sir Bruce. The number of staff was drastically reduced and some land was sold, but considering the circumstances the estate remained remarkably intact.

Miss Chichester never married and devoted her life to Arlington. The next 50 years were spent clearing her father's debts. Jan Newman, a trusted and loyal servant, remembered the day in 1928 when Miss Chichester paid off the last of the mortgages on the estate: 'We were given a great treat and sent to one of the shows at Barnstaple which were put on each year by the Operatic Company.'

Woolacombe

The family owned large areas of land around Woolacombe. An initiative to develop the Woolacombe estate into one of the most attractive seaside resorts in the West Country was unsuccessful due to insufficient funding.

Canon Rawnsley, one of the three founders of the National Trust, was a friend and in 1909, following her mother's death, Miss Chichester passed some of the land that they owned in this area to the National Trust. Parade House at Woolacombe was retained as a retreat of which Miss Chichester was particularly fond and it was here that she spent her final days.

Left Rosalie with one of the family's dogs

Right Parade House, photographed by Rosalie Chichester

A lifetime collecting

Miss Chichester had a lively interest in many aspects of life including art, music, inventions, astronomy and politics. She won prizes for photographs that she developed and printed herself and, along with many unpublished romantic novels, she wrote regularly for the *Daily Sketch*. Collecting memorabilia appeared to be a favourite pastime: shells, stamps, model ships, pewter, tea caddies, stuffed birds, greeting cards, jade, the list was endless. Jan Newman remembered that the hall was very different from the scene today with 'cases of stuffed birds, butterflies, a kangaroo, a large bear, great cases of albatross' and, on top of the cabinets, 'Famille Rose china, great dishes and vases, snakes and insects. I was enthralled with them all.'

World travel and wildlife

Miss Chrissy Peters came to Arlington in 1912 as a paid companion. She shared many of Miss Chichester's interests including inventions, art and music. With the debts now less pressing, they embarked on two world cruises. In 1921 they visited Australia and New Zealand. Miss Chichester was so impressed with the national parks they visited on their travels that she began opening Arlington grounds during the summer months.

From the clean, crisp landscape of the 19th century the estate developed a wilder look. Trees and shrubs left unpruned began to encroach onto the lawns surrounding the house. Unlike her father she did not support hunting and by the 1930s an iron fence extending eight miles had been erected to protect the deer. The park was grazed by a flock of Jacob sheep whose descendants still feed on the lush grassland today. All wildlife was protected, Polly her father's parrot was allowed to roam freely throughout the house, and peacocks would wander in through the French doors.

Gift to the nation

Miss Chichester gave much thought to the future of the estate that had been the family home for many centuries. She did not want it to be divided and sold, so she bequeathed Arlington and all of its estates to the care of the National Trust.

Miss Chichester's memorial urn stands overlooking the lake, one of her favourite places.

Left Rosalie Chichester (second from left) and her companion Miss Chrissy Peters (far left) photographed in New Zealand during their world tour in 1928

Above Rosalie at once in front of and behind the camera

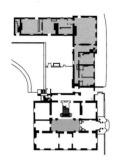

TOUR OF THE HOUSE

The harsh grey exterior of the house is in sharp contrast to the warm and intimate family home through the unusual curved doors. The small Entrance Hall displays a plaque of the family motto *Firm en Foi* – 'Firm in Faith' – and contains clues to the family's abiding passions for politics, sailing, animals and art, but the great surprise for the visitor is to be found upon entering the Staircase Hall.

THE STAIRCASE HALL

This large and dramatic Staircase Hall made a real statement as to the family's growing wealth and position. It was redesigned in 1865 by Sir Bruce Chichester to create a spacious area to feature the dramatic staircase. On either side of the lower steps are two brass signal cannons from the yacht *Erminia*. The wall space has been used to display a number of yachting pictures and a collection of model ships in their cases to reflect the family's love of sailing (see also page 26).

Right View of the Staircase Hall, *c.*1914, a watercolour by Miss Chichester's companion Chrissy Peters

Windows

The skylight lantern window originally provided the only light into an otherwise windowless room. In 1865, large arched windows were installed above the first landing. *The stained-glass heraldic shields* commemorate Chichester marriages from Sir John Chichester and Margaret Beaumont in 1505 to Sir Bruce's own marriage to Rosalie Chamberlayne in 1865.

Pictures

In the recessed area left of the staircase stands a *decoupage scrap screen*. This 18th-century screen is particularly interesting because most of the pictures are taken from fashionable caricatures of the day.

On the wall opposite the screen hangs a series of *watercolours by Miss Chrissy Peters*, Miss Chichester's companion. These paintings provide an insight into the way the house looked around 1914.

Right of the staircase hangs a *drawing of the intended suspension bridge at Arlington* signed by William Dredge, Civil Engineer 1849. These plans were abandoned on the death of Sir John Chichester in 1851.

Heating

Arlington still retains part of its original heating system thought to date around 1898. It is considered quite important and a rare example of its type. The original boiler is situated in the cellar and the remaining ornamental enclosures stand either side of the staircase.

Right Detail of the scrap screen in the Staircase Hall

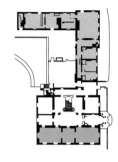

14

Thomas Lee designed this long room into three distinct areas punctuated by yellow scagliola Ionic columns. Each column stands proud of mirrored compartments containing hinged screens. The screens fold back to reveal a single room 70 feet long. Into this magnificent space seven windows shed their light onto the elegant décor and furnishings of the Morning Room, Ante Room and White Drawing Room.

Fortunately during the remodelling of 1865 Sir Bruce Chichester did not materially alter the decoration of the main reception rooms, which are in vivid contrast with the severity of the exterior. Lee's design of the dividing columns and screens, the handkerchief dome and segmental arches above the Ante Room show the influence of his mentor Sir John Soane.

Below

The Morning Room in use as a dining room

The un-restored ornate ceiling plasterwork of the Morning Room and Ante Room and their original wallpaper and wall hangings show the workmanship and designs of 1839. A hand-knotted Donegal carpet with the family crest of a heron in each corner was made in 1820 for the White Drawing Room. The carpet had become badly worn, and in 1978 the Trust was able to have an exact replica made from the original design.

The Morning Room

This room was originally designed as the dining room. The dumb waiters, hidden behind two painted panels, brought food up from the kitchen below – one is shown open. The wallpaper is probably French, the green Rococo pattern being cut out and applied to a lining paper allowing adjustments to fit the room. The fireplace is made from marble found near Ashburton in South Devon. When the new dining room was added, Sir Bruce changed the use to a reception room for morning visitors.

The Ante Room

Like the Morning Room, the décor remains largely unchanged since 1839 when Sir John Chichester employed London decorators John Crace and George Trollop to refurbish the house following his marriage the previous year. The crimson wallhangings are of Spitalfields silk. Behind the mirrored panels are adjustable bookshelves. During Sir Bruce's remodelling it became a reception area for guests while they waited to be received. The original entrance to this room is now used as a display cabinet.

The White Drawing Room

This formal room was designed for the ladies of the house to conduct their business in or to withdraw to after an evening meal. Miss Chichester was known to have loved this room where she could sit and watch her beloved canaries in their cages. Towards the end of her life she spent most of her time here reclining on the sofa in front of the magnificent fireplace made of burnished steel and Italian marble.

Collections

Throughout the tripartite Long Room many items are displayed from Miss Chichester's vast and varied collections. Shells became a fascination and she acquired many rare and unusual specimens, part of the collection is displayed in the Morning Room and there are

Below The White Drawing Room

cabinets full of shells around the house. Among the intriguing items in the tall display cabinet in the Ante Room is a *stirrup glass* used by mounted riders for their pre-hunt tipple. The White Drawing Room displays two items of great interest: a *Flemish psalter* dated to the 13th century and a finely carved *red amber elephant* of Chinese origin.

Conservation vs restoration

The National Trust sometimes has to make difficult decisions about whether to preserve or restore. The Morning and White Drawing Rooms are excellent examples of this challenge. Although the Morning Room may at first glance seem shabby and dirty, it is largely unchanged since the ceilings were painted in the 1850s. The White Drawing Room, on the other hand, was redecorated in 1982 and, although it may look attractive, tells us nothing except what happened to the room 30 years after the National Trust took it over. Sir Bruce's 1865 dining room was demolished by the Trust in the 1950s because it was structurally unsound and there was not the money to rescue it at the time. A restoration project would be expensive and lengthy, and in essence leave us with an attractive 'fake' that would actually tell us very little. Modern attitudes might take a different approach to those of the past, but this is all part of the difficulty in managing a historic property.

Right The Crace wallpaper hanging in the Morning Room, as seen in the photograph opposite taken before the remodelling

THE BOUDOIR

The Boudoir is beautifully balanced with the Entrance Hall. Its original plaster ceilings and faded rose-gold silk wall-hangings epitomise the elegance of Thomas Lee's design. The shallow domes, segmental arches and mirrored panels create a cosy retreat for the lady of the house.

A boudoir is designed as a lady's private sitting, dressing or bedroom. The word is derived from *bouder*, 'to sulk'. In later years this room was used as Miss Chichester's bedroom having easy access to the White Drawing Room nearby.

In common with the Entrance Hall and Portico Room, the creative use of a vaulted ceiling gives an illusion of space. This ceiling, with rosettes framed in mouldings of acanthus leaves, differs from other vaulted ceilings in the house by being decorated.

Furnishings

The red and gold silk wall-hangings, original to this room, are extremely fragile. Italianate pilasters stand either side of the mirrored recesses into which are placed *two Parian-ware figurines* made by Minton in 1848: 'Rape of the Sabines' left and 'Fate of Andromeda' right.

THE MUSIC ROOM

In around 1865 this room was used as a billiard room, but by the time the National Trust acquired Arlington in 1949 it was suffering from wood rot. Government restrictions on building works after the Second World War meant that not all restoration work could be carried out and the painted ceiling and papier maché fillet round the walls were lost. The room reportedly had musical motifs on its ceiling, hence it being named the Music Room.

Pictures

The painting of Bruce and Caroline Chichester as children is by John Edgar Williams (active 1846–83) and depicts Sir Bruce Chichester seated on a donkey held by his sister Caroline, later Lady Clay. Both children are wearing Maltese costume.

Opposite Double portrait of Bruce and Caroline Chichester; by J. Edgar Williams, 1849

Right A fire-screen would protect the face of the lady at repose in the Boudoir

Furnishings

Interconnecting doors, known as jib doors, enabled a degree of privacy by linking bedrooms and sometimes service areas. This reduced the visibility of servants, and family members if they so wished, in the Staircase Hall or on the gallery landings.

Personal effects

The two hats displayed in the room are known as busbies and are relics of Sir Bruce's service with the North Devon Yeomanry. The red bags attached to the hats could be joined to the soldier's shoulder as a defence against sabre cuts.

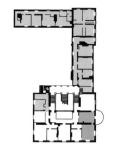

MISS CHICHESTER'S BEDROOM

Occupying a relatively private corner of the first floor with two large windows offering wonderful views over the estate and garden, this room has almost certainly been the master bedroom throughout the history of the house. Evidence suggests that this was a room favoured by the ladies of the house.

Originally known as the White Bedroom, it was here on 29 November 1865 that Lady Chichester gave birth to her daughter, Rosalie. After Lady Chichester vacated the room, it is not known if Miss Chichester ever slept here or whether she used it more as a boudoir.

Among the many items on display in the room is a silver dressing set owned by the family of Miss Chichester's godmother, Baroness von Klank – the curling tongs would be heated over a naked flame. The colourful quilt, dated around 1890 on the elegantly draped half-tester bed, also belonged to her godmother.

THE PORTICO ROOM

The Portico Room exactly mirrors the Entrance Hall directly below it, including a vaulted ceiling. This room was traditionally used as a gentleman's dressing room or bedroom. Sir Bruce died here in 1881, having moved into it to be nearer his wife during his long illness. There are fine views of the garden from the window.

Left The Portico Room enjoys fine views of the garden

Opposite Close-up of the dressing table in Miss Chichester's Bedroom

THE NURSERY

This room, set up by the National Trust to display Miss Chichester's childhood toys, originally served as the dressing room to the master bedroom. In keeping with social conventions of the time, Miss Rosalie Chichester as a young child would have been placed in the care of a nanny and the original nursery was probably situated across the landing.

Toys

The room contains many original items from Miss Chichester's young life. *The mahogany and wicker rocking cradle* was bought especially for her. Among the many toys displayed on shelves and surfaces are a beautifully made wooden tortoise, often mistaken for a real one, and two mice, Mina and Mineril, once her pets. On their death they were stuffed and mounted, quite accepted at the time and seen as a mark of affection. A string box and two pincushion holders were made from ivory by her maternal grandfather Thomas Chamberlayne.

Opposite The Library Bedroom

Below, right The Nursery

Below The toys on show include 'Monsieur Leotard', a Victorian trapeze artist, and 'George', a 1909 Steiff teddy

THE LIBRARY BEDROOM

A painting by Miss Peters shows two large bookcases on the landing and flanking the door, and this may have given rise to the naming of this room.

After her husband's death Lady Chichester took this room as her bedroom which was furnished with a gift of Italian furniture from her second husband, Sir Arthur Chichester. The furniture was sold by Miss Chichester after her mother's death in 1908.

Furnishings

The present furnishings have been brought in from elsewhere in the house. *The hand-sewn counterpane* was found rolled up in a drawer bearing a note stating that it was made by Mrs Page, maternal grandmother of the yachtsman Sir Francis Chichester. The richly decorated commode would have been seen as quite a status symbol. The term 'commode' in England has become associated with an item of furniture that contains a built-in chamber pot, however this is an example of an *18th-century French chest of drawers*.

Pictures

All of the photographs on display have a connection to Lady Rosalie Chichester including many of the Chamberlayne family.

THE DINING ROOM

This modestly sized room was originally used as the library but was made into a dining room sometime during the early 1900s. As a single lady, Miss Chichester was unlikely to be entertaining on a lavish scale and had no need for a large dining room. The other probable reason for this conversion was that she had begun to use her father's 1865 dining room as a museum for the many objects she was beginning to amass.

Furnishings

The Dining Room was redecorated in 1995 using wallpaper based on a 19th-century design by John Crace.

An interesting amalgamation of pieces makes up the striking fireplace. *The classical-style marble mantelpiece* is thought to be from the earlier 1790s house, although the central plaque has been replaced. The burnished steel surround is possibly original, while the iron fire-basket is a later addition and came from an outbuilding on the estate known as the Reading Room. The brass decoration is thought to have been added for Miss Chichester around 1920.

Opposite The white marble chimneypiece was salvaged from the former house in 1820

Changing rooms

In 1823 the service rooms and kitchens were hidden away in the basement of the original house. Sir Bruce, possibly considering this a fire risk, moved them in 1865 to the new service wing. The kitchens were now located in the far corner of the new wing. This photograph shows them in 1900. Today this is the Kitchen Tea Room. Unfortunately no sign of the 1865 kitchens exists. The basement has also been put to a different use and is the location of the bat hibernacula. Access is not permitted to the 1823 kitchens in the basement due to the presence of bats which are a protected species.

THE BEAUVAIS TAPESTRIES

On display in the Tapestry Room, originally a gentleman's bedroom known as the Blue Room, are four 18th-century tapestries possibly acquired by Colonel Chichester in the 1790s. It is thought that they were brought from one of the Welsh properties to be hung as grand wall-hangings in Sir Bruce's new dining room at Arlington. The National Trust cleaned and restored them to their full glory and since 1998 they have been displayed in their current location under dimmed lights to protect them from fading. The tapestries, woven with silk for highlights and wool as a soft contrast, have retained much of their rich colouring. Each tapestry illustrates one of four continents – Africa, America, Europe (above) and Asia – with added symbolism reflecting French ambitions at the time.

WILLIAM BLAKE

The painting by William Blake (1757–1827) is a unique find. Known as *The Sea of Time and Space* or *The Arlington Court Picture*, it is a watercolour drawing of an Old Testament scene, signed and dated by the artist. It is also believed to be the only Blake artwork in its original frame. It was found in 1949 covered in dust on top of a pantry cupboard and was believed to have been commissioned by Colonel John Palmer Chichester. However, it is also possible that it was a wedding gift from his third wife, Sophia Chichester née Ford, or possibly her mother, Lady Ford, in 1822. The frame-maker, James Linnell was known to Lady Ford, and he was an associate of Blake – this may have been the connection that led to the picture and frame being commissioned and given to Colonel John.

THE SHIP COLLECTION

Miss Rosalie Chichester was born into a family with a love of the sea. Her father, Sir Bruce, was a member of the Royal Yacht Squadron and owned two yachts, *Zoë* and *Erminia*. Her maternal grandfather, Thomas Chamberlayne, was also a keen yachtsman – his cutter *Arrow* was the most famous of all mid-19th-century racing yachts and the only British yacht to defeat the schooner *America* (after which the America's Cup is named). Miss Chichester brought the sea to Arlington with her collection of model ships, which was continually being increased by purchases through the London and local salesrooms. At the time of her death in 1949 she was the owner of a great collection of nautical miscellany.

French prisoner-of-war models
Arlington is fortunate to have 36 models in the collection made by French prisoners whilst held in British gaols during the Napoleonic Wars. Whilst living under extremely harsh conditions and with few tools and materials to hand, some incredible ship models were produced. There are examples of almost every class of ship of the Napoleonic War period, from great three deckers to smaller sailing frigates with their racing lines.

Dunkirk models
Miss Chichester's last commission, the Dunkirk Collection, was intended to commemorate the evacuation of Allied Troops from Occupied France in 1940. Only half of the collection was delivered, the second part of the order was cancelled by the National Trust after her death.

Gypsy Moth IV
The National Trust has added this yacht to the collection to commemorate the epic voyage of Sir Francis Chichester who sailed around the world in *Gypsy Moth IV*, being knighted upon his return. He was grandson of Sir Arthur Chichester, the second husband of Lady Chichester, making Miss Chichester his step-aunt.

Other models
Other models in the collection are made of bronze, glass, tortoiseshell, wood and bone. There are three- and four-masted ships, drifters, trawlers, frigates and a two-decker warship in a bottle. Today this collection is displayed in various locations around the house.

Top A model made by French POWs during the Napoleonic wars
Bottom Silver model of the *Gypsy Moth IV*, Sir Francis Chichester's yacht in which he circumnavigated the world in 1966–7

THE PEWTER COLLECTION

Miss Chichester's collection of approximately 400 pieces of pewter is the largest and most varied held by the National Trust and one of the finest on public view outside the major museums. A few pieces bear the arms of the Chichester family. Arlington is indebted to the Pewter Society for cataloguing and photographing the collection in 2000.

What is pewter?

Made of an alloy of tin, lead and copper and sometimes described as 'poor man's silver', pewter has been made into tableware and household items since the ancient Chinese and Roman periods some two thousand years ago. During the 18th century, as understanding grew of the poisonous qualities of lead, it was replaced with antimony which, when added to tin and copper, is more properly known as Britannia metal.

Continental

There are a few notable continental items, including a set of three 16th-century flagons found at Elunberg Castle in Bavaria and two rare French dishes dating from the late 16th century. The design on the Nurnberg Temperantia basin was cast in 1611 and later copied in silver to become the basin presented to the Wimbledon Ladies' Singles Champion.

British pewterware

The collection's strength is in pewterware from the British Isles. The earliest English pieces of the collection include a Romano-British ewer, a number of 16th-century spoons and an Elizabethan porringer with two clover-leaf ears. Among other notable pieces are English flagons, four very rare Stuart period candlesticks and a large collection of snuff boxes. The earliest Scottish piece is a pot-bellied measure from the late 17th century. One of the most interesting, and possibly unique, is a set of mid-19th-century thistle-shaped measures. They are rare because after they were issued it was discovered that they did not drain fully and should have been destroyed.

Top Nurnberg Temperantia basin cast in 1611

Bottom A Romano-British ewer, the oldest piece in the collection dating to *c.* AD 400

THE DESIGNED LANDSCAPE

Since Amyas Chichester settled at Arlington in the 16th century, the designed landscape has undergone several changes, from productive Tudor gardens to a 'picturesque' landscape which was further developed with 'gardenesque' features and Victorian style. In later years the gardens evolved as an environment for the nurture and protection of wildlife.

The Tudor house gardens

By the mid-18th century, the Tudor manor house was set in a series of garden enclosures bounded by a pair of symmetrical ornamental groves to the east. The gardens, which may have been terraced, descended to a series of partly ornamental orchards and fishponds in the valley to the west of the house known as the Wilderness.

Picturesque

Colonel Chichester transformed the grounds during the late 18th and early 19th centuries to provide a fashionable picturesque landscape for his newly modelled, late Georgian mansion. The garden enclosures were replaced with lawns planted with specimen trees and shrubs. Areas of parkland to the south and south-west replaced some of the agricultural land to create a natural-looking but aesthetically contrived vista. By damming two fishponds, the Wilderness Pond became a substantial water feature and new trees were planted in place of the orchards.

Gardenesque additions

By the mid-19th century a subtle and sophisticated landscape had been developed to form a suitable setting for the neo-Classical 1820s house. Walks and drives were carefully planned to provide a series of contrasting sensations and experiences. Open lawns allowed views to the wider landscape or to features such as the church tower, these views being framed by ornamental shrubberies and trees. A series of strategically placed incidents added interest, such as a flower garden, a walled garden, a pinery and an outer garden. Late Victorian influence is seen with the new formal layout of the Victorian Garden, an avenue of monkey-puzzle trees along the west drive and the obelisk in the south-east park erected to commemorate Queen Victoria's Golden Jubilee.

Picturesque vs gardenesque

According to John Loudon's publication *The Suburban Gardener and Villa Companion* (1838), the picturesque landscape was 'the imitation of nature in a wild state, such as the painter delights to copy', while the gardenesque represented 'the imitation of nature, subjected to a certain degree of cultivation or improvement, suitable to the wants and wishes of man'.

Development of the estate

Prior to 1790 the estate was a farmed rather than an ornamental landscape. In order to enhance the elegant three-storeyed Georgian house with its bay windows, Colonel Chichester embarked on extensive remodelling to introduce lawns and specimen trees around the house, a vista of parkland to the south and new planting in the Wilderness Valley. Hunting was one of Colonel Chichester's pleasures and he kept a pack of hounds. Thirty years later when Sir John inherited the neo-Classical mansion, the landscape and garden were developed along picturesque lines, fashionable at the time. He created the flower garden, the Wilderness Pond, the Wilderness Walk and he had the River Yeo dammed to create Arlington Lake. Sir John made the front drive to the north-west of the house in about 1850, but his vision to build a drive from an entrance at Woolley Lodge on the road to Barnstaple (now the A39) to the house was an ambitious project that was never completed. The plan was to zigzag through the wood and cross the lake over a new suspension bridge, a drawing of which hangs in the Staircase Hall. The pillars can still be seen today standing either side of the lake.

Below View of the east front of Arlington in 1845

THE VICTORIAN GARDEN

The Victorian Garden appears to have been developed by the early 19th century to replace the old garden enclosures of the Tudor house.

Sir Bruce Chichester changed the original informal planting for the Victorian setting much as it is seen today. From the entrance gate a pair of ornamental herons stands either side of the lower terrace steps, which ascend the central pathway to the conservatory on the top terrace where a similar heron adorns the middle apex. The smaller, more ornate conservatory replaced the original glasshouses which stretched along the whole back wall and was used for vines and probably for growing fruit. The conservatory is used to grow a variety of tender plants such as those brought back to England by the great Victorian botanical explorers who travelled to all parts of the continent in a quest to find the unusual and exotic.

The herbaceous borders flanking the path on the top terrace were designed by John Sales in 1976 in a semi-formal pattern to reflect the Victorian feel of the garden. Each of the other terraces has its own feature. From the conservatory the slate steps take you down terrace by terrace.

The first has circular basket beds filled with colourful annuals and iron frames supporting climbing cobaeas. The two *Araucaria auracana* (monkey-puzzle trees), native to Chile, are offspring of two that grew here in the 19th century, known locally as Gog and Magog.

Another flight of steps leads you down to an attractive fountain surrounded by arched trellises planted with honeysuckle and surrounded by beds of seasonal planting. The view across the pond encompasses the church

tower and the façade of Glebe House. The final flight of steps is flanked by a bank of brightly colourful Japanese azaleas.

THE WALLED KITCHEN GARDEN

The one-acre Walled Kitchen Garden, to the north of the Victorian Garden, was originally within easy reach of the Georgian house. The distance became more pronounced when the new house was built within a picturesque ideal where domestic activities were hidden from view. During the latter years of Miss Chichester's life, there was little need for such a large productive garden and it fell into disuse.

Volunteers play a vital role in the daily upkeep and management of the house and garden and it is thanks to their help that since 1990 the National Trust has slowly restored the vegetable garden: the walls have been re-capped, paths reinstated, the central dipping pond cleared and a lean-to greenhouse rebuilt. Fruit trees have been trained along the walls and a soft-fruit cage erected. Flowers are grown especially for display in the house and produce from the garden is used in the restaurant and sold in the shop.

To the rear of the Walled Kitchen Garden there are remains of a pinery. It was very popular to grow pineapples at country estates in the early 19th century. As fashions changed, the pinery became a fernery before finally falling from fashion and becoming quite neglected by the early 20th century.

Top left Traditional glass cloches

Top right Espaliered apple tunnel in the Walled Kitchen Garden

Above Some of the tools used by the team of dedicated staff and volunteers

Opposite The conservatory is a 20th-century replacement of the Victorian original which would have had additional wings on either side

THE PLEASURE GROUNDS AND PARK

A picturesque landscape depends for its effect on a series of carefully designed and often contrived views and vistas in which contrasts of light and shade and enhancement of the natural beauty of the broader landscape are of paramount importance.

Fortunately Colonel Chichester was able to create a peaceful and unique picturesque landscape with little contrivance by replacing unsightly farm buildings with open grazed parkland planted with specimen trees. The enlarged Wilderness Pond provided shimmering light, whilst Deerpark Wood and Woolley Wood to the south and south-west presented contrasting shade.

Thirty years later, with the new mansion relocated, additional landscaping was needed to create a pleasing vista from the house. More parkland was introduced and planting within the Pleasure Grounds was used to frame a series of designed views. A network of drives encouraged visitors to explore the grounds where strategically placed incidents added interest, such as a picturesque cottage ornee in Gothic style built in Lodge Plantation. This was demolished around 1930.

As well as adding a new stable block, Sir Bruce built Home Farm to create an incident at the apex of the west drive and an avenue of monkey-puzzle trees was planted in a similar way to those found at Lady Rosalie Chichester's family home at Cranbury Park, Hampshire.

Miss Chichester kept her father's formal garden largely intact but the wider garden was allowed to become overgrown with clumps of unpruned shrubbery forming around existing specimen trees. New walks were introduced within the Pleasure Grounds breaking up large areas of 19th-century lawns. Arlington's wildlife and her own birds and animals were the prime consideration for the environment, although financial restraints may also have played a part in the subsequent decline of land management during this period of time.

A piece of land to the west of the house, known as the Rabbit Pit, is where Miss Chichester's pet rabbits were kept. The Pheasantry, built in 1993 by the National Trust, replaced an original structure of 1887. A memorial to Vanguard and Memory, two dogs of the Chichester family, is located nearby. Memory (whose sleeping figure can be seen immortalised in marble in the Ante Room) survived his master Sir Bruce by just seven weeks.

The Wilderness Pond
The shimmering water of the pond not only lightens the landscape but its reflective surface mirrors the trees, pampas grass and shrubs planted around its banks. An attractive feature in its own right, the pond is an important part of the panoramic view from the house to the parkland beyond where an obelisk, to commemorate Queen Victoria's Golden Jubilee, provides a far distant focal point.

The Wilderness Walk
Immediately below the pond an overflow pool flows into a stream, which tumbles down through the woodland to the River Yeo below.

The Wilderness was originally planted as ornamental orchards during Tudor times. Today a pleasant walk through a planting of beech and conifer trees leads down to the lake.

A circular walk of about an hour's duration (shown on the fold-out at the back of this guidebook) commencing at the West Drive encompasses many features of the Pleasure Grounds.

Above Light breaks through the trees on to the Wilderness Pond

THE STABLES

This fine colonnaded stable block designed by R.D. Gould for Sir Bruce Chichester in 1864 bears the heron crest above the clock tower. Built on the site of the previous stables of the Tudor house to the east of the church, Sir Bruce's stables are arranged around two sides of a courtyard. We believe that the stables were never completed, as most stable yards were built as a quadrangle. Today the quadrangle is completed by a modern building designed by Anthony Harrison in 2003, which occupies the west side of the courtyard and is home to the Carriage Museum.

The stables are a well-planned and functional building. Much thought went into their layout and location, as it was recommended in *The Complete Horseman* (1795): '[The stables] should be in good air and upon hard, firm and dry ground; be situated upon an ascent that the urine, foul water or any wet may be conveyed away by trenches or sinks. There is no animal that delights more in cleanliness, nor is more offended at unwholesome favours than a horse.'

Most importantly the stables had to be large enough to accommodate the horses of visitors, as well as those of the family. The stables at Arlington could house sixteen horses. A wealthy family like the Chichesters would have kept a range of horses, some for riding and hunting, but perhaps only a couple for carriage driving.

Today the head coachman leads a small team of staff to manage the working horses that are stabled in the south-west corner of the stable block. They take it in turns to pull the carriage around the grounds. The horses' modern harness is cleaned and stored in the Harness Room, where it hangs alongside two sets of original 19th-century state harness. The stables team give daily demonstrations of harnessing.

The horses live outside and are brought into the stables to be fed and groomed. On their days off they can be found in the fields behind the house or opposite the church.

Carriage rides are available during opening hours, and private carriage driving experience days and lessons are offered from March to October.

Opposite Some of the residents of the stables at Arlington

Above Visitors can enjoy a carriage ride around the grounds

Right Harnesses and other pulling paraphernalia

THE NATIONAL TRUST CARRIAGE MUSEUM

The original nucleus of the collection of carriages at Arlington Court was a gift of eight carriages from the 7th Marquess of Bute in 1964. Since these carriages did not come from one of its houses, the National Trust had to decide where to display them. There were few stableyards that had not been converted into tea rooms, shops, toilets or accommodation, or a combination of these, either by the Trust or by the original owners of the properties. Of these it was decided that the most suitable was the yard at Arlington Court. Fortunately it is some way from the house and is not on the route that visitors take when they arrive and leave, or it would probably have been converted like so many others.

Carriages had become collectors' pieces and, as with so much else, American money soon sent values soaring. Many carriages were being rescued from decay and exported worldwide and the National Trust decided in 1966 to create a representative collection of British carriages. A gift of three carriages soon followed from the executors of the late Sir Dymoke White, and a loan of seven carriages came from the Science Museum. Although none of the carriages belongs to Arlington Court, three have come from other National Trust houses.

Despite the partitions and furniture in two ranges of stables being removed to accommodate the carriages, and with the smaller carriages on display in the original hay loft, the collection soon outgrew the available space. In 2003, a modern extension was built but even now there is insufficient space and new loans and gifts often have to be refused.

Carriages through the ages

Following the departure of the Romans no good roads were built in Britain for approximately 1,500 years. Although carriages, as we understand them today, were introduced in Elizabethan times, they were only used by royalty and the wealthiest of the nobility until the 18th century. Even then they were principally used for occasions of state and seldom used for long distance travel because the condition of the roads made this

Above The crest of the 7th Marquess of Bute on his single brougham

Classes of carriage

The appeal and requirement for a carriage was summarised by Frank Huggett in *Carriages at Eight* (1979) when he wrote: 'Wealthy aristocrats needed seven or eight carriages to preserve their distinction from the rising middle classes and to provide a suitable vehicle for every aspect of their busy social life; professional men needed a carriage for themselves and another for their wives; middle-class ladies of humble origins wanted to drive out in a carriage in the afternoons to impress their friends and neighbours; young men needed a carriage to interest young ladies, and even the servants in big houses wanted to have unauthorised use of a carriage, when the family was out of town, to take their kitchen guests back to their basements.'

impractical. Towards the end of the 18th century, these conditions improved. A large number of different carriage types were developed and the carriage building trade began to expand and prosper.

Road engineers such as Thomas Telford and John Loudon McAdam dramatically improved the main roads in the early 19th century making the 'Golden Age' of coaching possible. Public transport in the form of royal mail coaches and stage coaches ran between all major towns and cities, and the British coaching system quickly became the envy of the world and was subsequently copied in many countries.

During the 19th century the ownership and use of carriages greatly increased. This was principally due to the improvement of the roads, which enabled carriages to be built much smaller, lighter and therefore cheaper; the technical advances of this industrially exciting period; and the spread of wealth to the ever increasing middle classes.

The so-called 'Golden Age' was very short because, by the time the main roads had been improved, the steam train was already on the drawing board. As the rail network expanded, coaching was driven into the remote areas not yet served by branch lines.

Coaching declined after the advent of the railways in the early 19th century, but it was not until the motor car became affordable to the masses that carriages became redundant in the early 20th century.

An almost bewildering variety of horse-drawn carriages existed. Arthur Ingram's *Horse Drawn Vehicles since 1760 in Colour* lists 325 types with a short description of each. A somewhat shorter list is available on loan to visitors to the Museum or to download from Arlington Court's web page, and a selection from the collection is presented on the pages that follow.

Below *Gentlemen's Carriages: A Cabriolet*, c.1820–30 (oil on canvas), Charles Hancock (1802–77)

Below All set for an outing in the family carriage

THE COLLECTION

Carriages of the wealthy

During the 19th century most aristocratic families owned a palatial London home in addition to their country houses. Their state or dress carriages were kept in the mews behind the house and only used for receptions, state occasions and other formal ceremonies. The barouche was used to take the air in the park, see society and perhaps more importantly, to be seen in. In order to travel between their properties these families generally owned travelling carriages. These were also suitable for long-distance foreign travel, such as the Grand Tour of the cultural cities of Europe.

Coachman-driven carriages

During the 19th century many more families could afford to employ servants, so a large proportion of carriages were coachman-driven. These were the principal carriages of the professionals and the middle-class families, and they were also the everyday carriages of the aristocracy and the wealthy, who continued to use their grander and more formal carriages when the occasion demanded.

Owner-driven carriages

People who could not afford to employ a coachman obviously had to drive themselves. However, once the Prince of Wales, the future King George IV, and his circle of friends discovered the pleasures of driving it became a fashionable sport. This trend continued throughout the 19th century and many carriage types were developed for the country sportsman and for driving in the park.

Informal carriages

These carriages were generally found on the country estates and were extremely versatile. It was socially acceptable for these carriages to be driven either by the owner or by his professional coachman. They were based on the open wagonette style, with the seats arranged along the length of the carriage, facing in, and various methods were devised to provide shelter from the weather.

Carriages for other uses

A number of private carriages were produced that do not easily fit into the groups already described. These include little carriages intended for mothers or governesses to take the air with the children and miniature carriages intended to be pulled by children, dogs or goats. There were also carriages developed for use by invalids and the elderly. The only commercial vehicles in the collection are vehicles for carrying paying passengers around town, like the Hansom cab, or to their graves, like the hearse.

Top A Portland wagonette, late 1800s

Middle A park drag

Bottom A governess cart, early 1900s

OPPOSITE

Top A travelling coach

Middle A double brougham, 1893

Bottom A four-wheeled dog cart, with a rear boot for transporting small hunting dogs

THE STABLES TEAM

Keeping the wheels turning was a laborious task for men, boys and horses. A wealthy aristocratic family would have employed a number of experienced staff to run their stable yard, including a head coachman, possibly one or more under coachmen, and various grooms and stable boys. The hierarchy of the stables team was as strict as any within the house, and all looked to the head coachman to run the show.

The coachman

In a wealthy stables, the head coachman held the position of authority, managing his team of staff including under-coachman, groom to stable boy. He was usually provided with accommodation, an annual salary and an allowance for a full set of livery. It would be expected that he, the carriage and the horses would be turned out to perfection at any time of the day or night.

The groom

The groom was responsible for saddling or harnessing, feeding and watering the horses and oiling their harness. In large establishments he would answer to the head groom and might accompany a carriage to look after the horses. He would also receive accommodation, an annual salary and a full set of livery.

The stable boy

Bottom of the labour force and probably the most hard-worked of the team, the stable boy would be given the least desirable of tasks such as mucking out the horses and fetching and carrying for everyone. With large families and few working opportunities, a young boy was considered fortunate to be fed, clothed and given sleeping quarters in the stables and the chance to develop a career with horses.

Left Portrait of a coachman (oil on canvas), George Garrard (1760–1826)

Right Coachman's apparel

Opposite *A phaeton with a pair of cream ponies in the charge of a stable boy, c.1780–5 (oil on panel), George Stubbs (1724–1806)*

MAKING A JOURNEY

Above *The Exeter Royal Mail on a country road*, James Pollard (1792–1867)

Stage coaches and royal mail coaches

Until the advent of the railways, the majority of people who could afford to travel used the stage and royal mail coaches. The first stage coaches ran in the mid-17th century but because of the appalling state of the roads, they were painfully uncomfortable, slow and unreliable. The situation slowly improved and during coaching's Golden Age over 3,000 stages served all the principal towns in the country. They carried four inside passengers, twelve outside passengers and their entire luggage. Only the very best stage coaches could match the speed of the royal mail coaches, introduced in 1782, which only carried three outside passengers and had the advantage of an armed guard. The mail coaches left London at eight o'clock every evening and travelled through the night to the most important cities, and the mail was carried from there to the smaller towns. In 1837 it took sixteen and a half hours to travel from London to Exeter by mail coach at an average speed of about ten and a half miles per hour, including stops for meals and to change horses. They were changed every ten to twelve miles and the stops were so short that there was not even time to climb down from the coach. The only longer stop was for breakfast at Ilminster, where only 25 minutes were allowed.

Private travelling carriages

Stage coaches and mail coaches ran to a strict timetable so passengers could not choose the route, the time or their companions. By contrast, the wealthy were able to travel in their own comfortable private travelling carriages, choose their route and timetable, and stop whenever they wanted. Their servants would pack the imperials, budgets and other cases and strap them in place on the carriage, and a valet and a lady's maid were generally carried in the external rumble seat behind the carriage body. They made use of the posting system, whereby pairs or teams of horses, ridden postillion by postboys, were hired from posting inns along the route. Some of these carriages incorporated a dormeuse boot to enable the occupants to lie at full length and rest during the journey; Venetian blinds that could be raised in place of the windows to control the ventilation; a sword case to carry not only swords but also umbrellas, parasols and walking sticks; and wells beneath the floor containing all that could be needed on the journey, accessible through trap hatches.

Foreign travel

The success of the Grand Tour or any other foreign journey depended on a courier who was commissioned to travel in the saddle with the party. Dressed smartly and generally with knowledge of three or four languages, he would organise the route, determine the length of the day's journey, ride ahead to arrange relays of post-horses, order rooms at hotels, settle bills, pay all the expenses on the road and duly render periodical accounts of money supplied to him. If the tour was prolonged – it was not uncommon to last over a year – an additional vehicle called a fourgon, which could also carry servants, was sometimes used so that even more clothes and other luggage could be carried.

Left Coach travellers taking breakfast at an inn. Outside the coachman tries to keep warm in the cold morning air

THE ESTATE TODAY

Arlington estate is a wonderfully tranquil place having changed little over the last 200 years when the impressive park landscape was introduced by Colonel John Chichester and further developed by his son Sir John Chichester.

Grazing and farming

When the National Trust acquired Arlington in 1949 the estate comprised eighteen farms. Today, six tenanted farms support dairy and stock-rearing enterprises on predominately rolling pastureland enclosed by typical Devon banks and hedges. Farm buildings and machinery have been modernised and land management techniques introduced in accordance with agricultural practices required by today's farming industry.

Today the National Trust manages the main park with its own Devon cattle and Jacob sheep. Grazing helps to keep grass manageable, brambles at bay and encourages the growth of wild flowers. In its heyday the parklands would have been planted with more trees than are left today and a programme of planting has already commenced with native oak, lime, ash and beech. More exotic trees, such as Corsican pine and Scots pine, have also been planted. These were species favoured by the Victorians.

The woodlands

The woodlands at Arlington are extensive and of great importance in terms of landscape preserved and wildlife supported. Much of the woodland area is broadleaved and ancient in origin, with parts traceable to the Domesday survey of 1086.

Conifers were introduced to the woodlands in the late 1940s to provide timber for buildings and domestic use. The long-term objective is to replace these with oak and ash, the oak being regenerated naturally from seed whenever possible. It is costly to fell trees, so the timber is used for fencing and sold for pulp, and in the future it will fuel a heating system for the house.

As at many other large estates, the *Ponticum rhododendron* planted during the Victorian era has proved to be very invasive, leaving little room for wild flowers and vegetation to grow on the woodland floor. Laurel shrubs are not quite as invasive but still need a great deal of management to keep them under control.

Access

The drives, built for carriage and horses, are still used for that purpose today as visitors can

Opposite

Right The lake was created in 1837 by damming the Yeo

Left Miss Chichester's memorial urn was from a design by Robert Adam

Right Jacob's sheep grazing on the estate

enjoy a horse-drawn tour of the estate. The drives also allow access for working vehicles and more importantly for visitors to enjoy the many features of the gardens and Pleasure Grounds on foot. New footpaths have been opened and walkers can explore many miles of beautiful, peaceful countryside. Over recent years three miles of new bridleway have been introduced to enable horses to be ridden through the estate to the lake.

The wetlands

The lake was created in 1837 by damming the River Yeo. By the 1930s the upper lake was overgrown with willow. A major dredging operation was carried out in 2000, but silting continues to be a problem. Not only is dredging difficult and expensive, but there are also serious environmental issues relating to disposal of the waste.

It is here on the north-east shore of this peaceful haven that Miss Chichester chose to have her ashes buried beneath a memorial urn designed by Robert Adam.

ARLINGTON'S WILDLIFE

The parkland, woodlands, wetlands and gardens are a haven to a wide variety of wildlife and the protection and active conservation of their habitats is the major objective of the management of the estate today.

By the mid-20th century the condition of the grounds had declined, as maintenance was not undertaken. Miss Chichester loved nature and preferred a wilder environment for the estate's flora and fauna. Since the National Trust inherited the estate in 1949, work has been undertaken to ensure that the grounds are safe and attractive for visitors and are effectively managed with conservation and biodiversity as a priority.

A natural woodland of new growth, mature trees and those that are dead and dying provides a habitat for a wide range of birds, animals and invertebrates. The good air quality of North Devon is a factor in enabling lichen to grow exceptionally well, so much so that the area has been declared a Site of Special Scientific Interest (SSSI) on account of its rare and unusual species.

Woodland butterflies flourish and a small area provides vegetation for the rare marsh fritillary butterfly. Wild red deer and roe deer are a common sight and, although rarely spotted, the dormouse and otter have been recorded at Arlington.

Bats in the balance

Conservationists consider that the future of the seventeen species of bats resident in the British Isles is in the balance, fewer more precariously than the lesser horseshoe bat, which has declined by 90 per cent during the past 100 years. Arlington is fortunate to have 150–170 lesser horseshoe bats, which can be viewed in the roof of the house by a 'batcam' during the summer. Many other species roost in trees, under bridges, in sheds and in virtually all of the houses and cottages on the estate. To assist with the conservation of bats, old trees are retained and deadwood is allowed to stand.

Lake dwellers

The River Yeo, the lake and the Wilderness Pond all provide for water- and wetland-loving flora and fauna. The otter frequents the River Yeo and, like the herons nesting in the high trees on the far side of the lake, they feed on trout and other freshwater fish. Water birds

OPPOSITE

Top left Two marsh fritillary butterflies (*Euphydryas aurinia*)

Bottom left Lesser horseshoe bat (*Rhinolophus hipposideros*)

Right and main picture opposite Lichens and mosses growing on trees. The lichen thrives here because the air is so moist and clean

such as teal, pochard and tufted ducks enjoy the calm water of the lake. An occasional flash of blue of a kingfisher rewards some visitors, and dippers are often see at the lake. Pied flycatchers are regular migrants to the oak woodlands near the river and lake.

ARLINGTON'S FUTURE

Arlington Court has for hundreds of years been the backdrop for the dramatically changing fortunes of the Chichester family. The formal, walled and wilderness gardens have evolved with the passing fashions. Miss Chichester's benign neglect is now superseded by the National Trust's active conservation.

The estate will continue to develop and it is the challenge enthusiastically accepted by the team of staff and volunteers at Arlington Court to conserve this gift and share it with as many as want to enjoy it. The landscape visualised by Colonel Chichester is not seen to be in conflict with the wildlife park so dear to Miss Rosalie Chichester. With careful management, the ideals of both of these visionary members of the family can be encompassed, in the same way that the picturesque is not about taming nature but about using it as a rustic context for the landscape. Active conservation and wildlife biodiversity are central to decisions relating to any changes or new developments at Arlington Court, all the while ensuring that this unspoilt corner remains open and accessible for ever and for everyone.

Left The direction of Arlington's future is clear.